Write Your Own Will

Write Your Own Will

ROBERT J. SCHWARTZ

MEMBER OF THE NEW YORK BAR

revised edition

COLLIER BOOKS

A Division of Macmillan Publishing Co., Inc.

NEW YORK

COLLIER MACMILLAN PUBLISHERS

LONDON

Contents

Introduction   13
Age Requirements (Minimum and Maximum)   17
Who Should Not Use This Book   23
The Form of Your Will   27
Canceling a Previous Will   29
Your Debts and Funeral Expenses   31
Gifts of Specific Items   33
Gifts of a General Nature   35
Charitable Bequests   37
Residual Clauses   39
Selecting Your Executor   41
What Do You Want Your Executor to Do?   45
Closing Your Will   47
Attestation of Your Will   49
The Actual Signing and Execution of Your Will   53
After Your Death   55
Changing Your Will   57
If Your Estate Does Not Have Enough Assets   61
Property Which Cannot Be Transferred by a Will   63
Problems of Disinheritance (Wife or Husband)   67
Problems of Disinheritance Continued (Children and
    Others)   71
Problems of Disinheritance Continued (Community
    Property States)   75
Release of Obligation Owing to You   77
The Question of Survivorship and Lapsed Legacies   79
Preventing Litigation Involving Your Estate   83
Illegal Bequests   87
Encumbered Property   91

Tax Avoidance on Your Estate   93
Some Duties of an Executor (a partial list)   97
Questions and Answers   99
Additional Clauses Which May Be Suitable for
    Certain Wills   103
Federal Estate Taxes   108
New York State Inheritance Rates   110
State Tax Credit   112
A Few Sample Wills   113

Write Your Own Will

Introduction

Please read this—it is important

THIS BOOK is an outline of how to write your will. After you have understood this book, you yourself will be able to prepare your own will.

No book can hope to take the place of a lawyer, and this one makes no pretensions in the direction. It should be kept in mind that the services of an experienced lawyer are unique. Reading through this book, however, will acquaint you with all of the problems you will ordinarily encounter in will-making.

The first part of the book briefly sets forth the essential parts of an ordinary will. Thereafter there are sections on changing your will, property which you cannot transfer by will, disinheritance, community property and how to save on inheritance taxes. You should read *all* of this book before you sit down to write your will.

The fact that you have purchased this book indicates your understanding of the great need for every living person to have a will. Laws have been passed in all of the states providing for the disposition of your property, if you should die without leaving a will. And yet, it is an unusual person who is aware of what disposition will be made of his property, should he die without leaving a will. In very many cases, the disposition provided by law would not represent your choice. After your death, there is absolutely nothing that you can do about it, but right now you can control the disposition of your property by means of a legal document that we all know as a WILL.

You can draw your own will

It is the purpose of this book to teach you how to write your own will. Step by step, you can complete this document so that your property will be distributed in accordance with your wishes. You yourself can draw such an instrument with no outside assistance, and it will be binding and effective. Your wishes will be carried out precisely as you direct. The more care and attention that you give to the material presented herein, the more binding and effective your will can be.

Just one word of caution. Please do not glance through the book hastily and then feel that you are qualified to draw your will. Read every word of every section, so that you may gain every possible benefit.

You may typewrite your will, or you may use pen and ink. Do not use a pencil. A good suggestion is to prepare a draft of your will using plain paper. Make your corrections, and then copy the corrected draft onto the form provided at the end of this book.

Make no corrections

Remember this: In your final copy, do not make any corrections, even slight ones. The laws do not permit crossing out, erasing, or otherwise correcting ANYTHING contained in your will. It must be an absolutely PERFECT copy.

Now, go ahead and read the book. Please read carefully so that you absorb as much as possible. When you have finished you should be able to write your own will with no difficulty whatsoever.

Age Requirements (Maximum and Minimum)

In general, you should be 21 years of age in order to execute a will. However, there are a good many exceptions and these will be considered, so that if you are under the age of 21, you may nevertheless be able to write your will. In addition, a further distinction is drawn as to age requirements with regard to *real* property and *personal* property. But before we discuss the problem of the minimum age requirement, let us determine the difference between *real* and *personal* property:

Real and Personal property

Real property may be briefly described as land and buildings. *Personal* property consists of any property other than real property. For example, clothes, automobiles, mortgages, promissory notes, stocks and bonds, are all classified as personal property. On the other hand, any structure whether used for farming, offices, or a home, is considered real property. Most of the furniture in a building is held to be personal property. It is important to keep this distinction in mind in using the following table.

Assume that you are under the age of 21, and wish to make a will. This table lists the MINIMUM age re-

Minimum Age Requirements for Executing a Will

State	MALES		FEMALES	
	Real	Personal	Real	Personal
Alabama	21	18	21	18
Alaska	21	21	21	21
Arizona	21*	21*	21*	21*
Arkansas	18	18	18	18
California	18	18	18	18
Colorado	21	17	21	17
Connecticut	18	18	18	18
Delaware	21	21	21	21
Dist. of Col.	21	21	18	18
Florida	18	18	18	18
Georgia	14	14	14	14
Hawaii	20	20	20	20
Idaho	18	18	18	18
Illinois	18	18	18	18
Indiana	21	21	21	21
Iowa	21	21	21	21
Kansas	21	21	21	21
Kentucky	21	21	21	21
Louisiana	16	16	16	16
Maine	21	21	21†	21†
Maryland	21	21	18	18
Massachusetts	21	21	21	21
Michigan	21	21	21	21
Minnesota	21	21	21	21
Mississippi	21	21	21	21
Missouri	21	18	21	21
Montana	18	18	18	18
Nebraska	21	21	21	21
Nevada	18	18	18	18
New Hampshire	18*	18*	18*	18*
New Jersey	21	21	21	21
New Mexico	21	21	21	21
New York	21	18	21	18

Minimum Age Requirements for Executing a Will
(Continued)

	MALES		FEMALES	
State	Real	Personal	Real	Personal
North Carolina	21	21	21	21
North Dakota	18	18	18	18
Ohio	21	21	21	21
Oklahoma	18	18	18	18
Oregon	21	21	21	21
Pennsylvania	21	21	21	21
Puerto Rico	14	14	14	14
Rhode Island	21	18	21	18
South Carolina	21	14	21	12
South Dakota	18	18	18	18
Tennessee	18	18	18	18
Texas	21*	21*	21*	21*
Utah	18	18	18	18
Vermont	21	21	21	21
Virginia	21	18	21	18
Washington	21§	21§	21§	21§
West Virginia	21	21	21	21
Wisconsin	21	21	21‡	21‡
Wyoming	21	21	21	21

* Or married.
† Or married woman or widow.
§ Or married and over eighteen.
‡ Or married woman over eighteen.

quirement in each state for males and females, with regard to *real* and *personal* Property.

Legal residence determines minimum age requirements

Now, let us review the table of minimum age requirements. First of all, the state in which you regularly live is your legal residence, and you must satisfy the requirements of that state as to minimum age. This is important: You cannot evade this matter of age by writing your will in another state with lower age requirements, if you are only in such other state temporarily, or for a visit. For example, suppose that you are a resident of New York State and are 17 years old. You were born in New York City, and ordinarily live with your family in New York City. While attending college in Louisiana, you learn that the minimum age requirement there is only 16, so you execute a will in that state. However, your will is invalid, since you are a resident of New York, and therefore must comply with New York's higher age requirements as shown in the table. Unless you have given acceptable evidence of an intention to make Louisiana your legal residence, the law assumes that you will return to New York State, and therefore considers you a legal resident of that state.

Normal home address is your legal residence

Remember that for all practical purposes your normal home address is your legal residence and you must comply with the laws in that state in order to execute a valid will.

You will note that certain states listed in the table provide that any person who is married, even though under the age of 21, may execute a will. These states are Arizona, New Hampshire, Texas, and, if over 18, Washington. Wisconsin's reduction of the minimum age requirement applies only to married women, not to married men. Maine permits married women or widows under 21 to execute wills, but not married men or widowers under 21.

Therefore, do not attempt to execute a will if you do not meet the requirements of your state as to age. Nor does it help if you write a will when you are fairly close to the birthday that will bring you up to the minimum. For example, suppose you live in Indiana, which has a minimum age requirement of 21. Let us suppose that in twenty days you will be 21. Your will is invalid. And furthermore, it will be invalid, even when you have long since passed your 21st birthday. The reason is that if your will was invalid at the time you made it, nothing can make it valid.

Special provisions regarding real property

Suppose further that in your will you wish to leave real estate to someone, and this real property is located in a state other than the state in which you reside. It is necessary to examine the above table and see what the minimum age requirements are *in the state in which the real property is located*. For example, you are a resident of the state of Utah, which has an age requirement of 18 years. You are the owner of some farmland in Vermont. Let us further suppose that you are 20 years old. You will be permitted to execute a will as to both real and personal property in your home state of Utah, but you may not convey your real estate in Vermont, since you have not complied with Vermont's requirement that you be 21 years old before you can transfer real property by will in that state. On reaching the age of 21, you will be permitted to execute a will covering the Vermont real property.

No maximum age requirements

Until now, we have concentrated on the minimum age requirements. But is there a MAXIMUM age at which you are no longer permitted to write your will? Generally not, because the problem here is not one of age, but of the ability of the person who is writing the will to understand just exactly what he or she is doing. You may be 95 years old but if you are in full command of your faculties, you have an absolute right to execute a will. On the other hand, a man of 40 might lack the capacity to understand the nature of what he is doing in making a will.

Who Should Not Use This Book

The courts have decided that certain groups of persons are not qualified to execute wills. These include anyone who actually lacks the capacity to understand the nature of a will. Anyone confined to a mental institution, for instance, would not be considered qualified to decide for himself about the disposition of his property. The lunatic in an insane asylum is easily recognized as a problem.

Persons of extreme age

Much more difficult problems are presented by people of greatly advanced age who may or may not be too feeble-minded to execute a will. Because of the many legal complications facing very aged people, they should have their wills prepared for them by an attorney. It is always advisable to have an attorney prepare the will of such a person, particularly when it can be anticipated that the will may be attacked in court. The usual grounds for such an attack are that the person making the will lacked the mental capacity.

Divorced persons

If you were married but have in your hands a valid decree of divorce, then you have no special problem.

You may follow the instructions in this book, and draw your own will. This is true whether you have remarried or not.

If you are married but are separated from your husband or wife, you should read carefully the section entitled "Disinheritance (wife or husband)."

Married women

A common misapprehension among certain people is that a married woman may not prepare and execute a will without the consent of her husband. While this was true many years ago, it is no longer the law, and a married woman is as free as her husband to dispose of her property by will.

Aliens

Aliens may prepare their own wills and validly execute them. An alien may be briefly described as a person in the United States who is not a citizen.

Convicts

Convicts are customarily permitted to make wills even while under sentence for a crime.

In review, remember that the wills of those who lack the mental capacity to execute them will be set aside by law. Divorced persons may execute valid wills. Married women, aliens, and convicts can make valid wills.

Avoid freakish wills

At this time, a word of caution about the preparation of your will. Do not put in any freakish clauses, or request your executor to do any ridiculous things. It might result in your will being set aside. If you are angry with someone, do not use your will as a place to register your feeling. It is not the proper place since all that you are supposed to do when you make your will is dispose of your worldly goods.

The Form of Your Will

There is no required form of opening a will. However, custom has developed over the centuries, so that in substance, a certain pattern is followed. Accordingly, you will commence in the following fashion:

Opening clause

"In the name of God, Amen. I, John Thomas Martin of the City of Miami, County of Dade, State of Florida, being of sound mind and memory, but also aware of the uncertainties of this life, do hereby make, publish and declare this instrument as and for my LAST WILL AND TESTAMENT."

If you are an atheist, or are not of a religious turn of mind, you may completely dispense with the opening sentence. Thus, your will would begin: "I, John Thomas Martin ... etc."

Opening clause for those who have changed their names or residences

Special problems are presented in connection with those persons who have changed their names, or who have moved from their home town to a new community where they are little known. The latter situation might be of particular importance to elderly persons who have lived all their lives in one town, and then, upon retiring, move to a place where they know few people and live a secluded life. In that case, it is advisable to have an introductory clause as follows:

"In the name of God, Amen. I, Frederick William Corbett, formerly known as Frederick William Cribowicz, of the City of Los Angeles, County of Los Angeles, and State of California, but formerly residing at 969 East 87th Street, New York City, New York State, being of sound mind and memory but aware of the uncertainties of this life, do hereby make, publish and declare this instrument as and for my LAST WILL AND TESTAMENT."

Canceling a Previous Will

It is possible that you have made a will at one time or another. Whatever the reason, if you have even the slightest belief that this previous will is in existence, or if there is a possibility of its being in existence, it is advisable to indicate that you wish the previous will canceled.

Even if you have never had a previous will

In fact, it is advisable for you to insert the following clause even if you have never had a previous will. This will definitely prevent anyone from raising this question after your death. A simple clause is all that is needed but it may assist your executor a great deal. It should read as follows:

"I hereby revoke all testamentary instruments heretofore made and executed by me."

Your Debts and Funeral Expenses

Upon your decease, all of your obligations unpaid at that time, as well as your funeral expenses, must be met out of your estate, so you really have no choice in the matter of the next clause. However, it is a good idea to include it as a matter of form. This clause should read as follows:

"I hereby instruct my Executor to pay my just debts and funeral expenses, as soon after my death as may be practicable."

No particular creditor may be preferred

Do not include any instructions about which creditor is to be paid first even if you have reason to think there will not be enough assets to pay off your just debts. You are not the one to decide this. Each state has its own laws classifying creditors in order of priority.

Funeral instructions

If you have particular instructions you wish to leave to your executor concerning your funeral, this is the proper place for them. For example, if you wish to be cremated, or to be buried in a particular cemetery, or to have a monument placed over your grave, you should include instructions in your will. Here is an example of detailed instructions:

"I hereby instruct my Executor to pay my just debts and funeral expenses as soon after my death as may be practicable. I further order my Executor to have my body taken to the Simmons Funeral Home in Roanoke, Virginia, and to have my burial take place at our family cemetery plot in Lake Drive Funeral Park."

Suppose you own a particular piece of jewelry or some other valuable that you wish to leave to your daughter. This is known as a *specific bequest*. It is advisable to make a simple statement of your wishes, along these lines:

"I give, devise and bequeath to my daughter, Jane, the emerald necklace which has been in our family for over fifty years."

"I give, devise and bequeath to my son, Raymond, the house located at 316 E. Front Street, Riverview, New Jersey, together with all of the furniture and fixtures contained therein."

Be precise in describing real estate

If you are giving real property to a beneficiary, be careful to give the precise description of the real property in your will so that there can be no doubt of your intentions or of the location of the property. Of course, if the real estate is located in a city, an address is usually sufficient. But if the property is located in the country or consists of farm land, much greater care is advised. Do not describe property by calling it ". . . my farm land on the east side of the hill . . .". If it later appears that the property is located on the *north*-east side of the hill, your estate may be put to considerable trouble and expense to interpret your true meaning. Obtain a survey description and be safe.

Avoid possibility of confusion

However, caution is to be employed if you have any reason to suspect that there will be some confusion in identifying the item in question:

"I give, devise and bequeath to my son, Edward, the gold stickpin with rubies; the other gold stickpin without precious stones, I will dispose of in a subsequent bequest."

A thought that may arise in your mind is the possibility that the piece of property which you are setting forth in your specific bequest may have been exchanged for another similar property before your death. In that case it may be advisable to word the clause as follows:

"I give, devise and bequeath to my nephew, Andrew Warden, my automobile of any make whatsoever, of which I happen to be the owner at the time of my death."

Disposal of subject of bequest during your lifetime

Another likelihood is that you may have completely disposed of the subject of a specific bequest before your death, even though you owned it at the time of the execution of your will. The following wording will cover that possibility:

"I give, devise and bequeath to my good friend, Joseph Malden, the oil painting by the artist, Franz Hals, which is in my library, provided, however, that I am the owner of such oil painting at the time of my death."

If you think that the person you are naming as a beneficiary cannot readily be located by your executor, you should place that person's address after his name.

Gifts of a General Nature

General bequests, or general legacies differ somewhat from specific bequests. Remember that in the specific type of bequest you were giving a particular thing, which you carefully described in order to avoid confusion. However, a general bequest is one in which property is paid to a beneficiary out of your general estate. The general bequest is usually a sum of money and is regarded as general since it is paid out of the general assets of your estate. This is easily handled in your will by this simple paragraph:

"I hereby give, devise, and bequeath to my best friend, Herbert Patton, of 2415 Hawthorne Road, Phoenix, Arizona, the Sum of One Thousand ($1,000.) Dollars Cash."

Charitable Bequests

You may want to leave money to your church, college, or favorite charity.

Learn exact name of charity

It is of the utmost importance that you learn the exact name of the group or organization to benefit from your will. Some charities are incorporated, some are not. Make sure the gift reaches the right charity by giving its correct name. It is advisable at the same time to find out if the charity is permitted to receive gifts for the purpose you have in mind. Here are examples of a few such clauses:

"I give, devise and bequeath the sum of Five Thousand ($5,000.) Dollars to the Johnson County Hospital located in Johnson County, Texas."

"I give, devise and bequeath the sum of Twenty Five Hundred ($2500.) Dollars to the Trustees of the University of Pennsylvania, Philadelphia, Pennsylvania, for the purpose of purchasing books on chemistry for the library of that university, in the sole discretion of said trustees of the university."

Limit on charitable bequests

If you have a wife or children, many states will not permit you to leave to charity more than one-third or one-half of your estate. Check the laws of your state, should you desire to give more than a third of your estate to charity.

Residual Clauses

You have now reviewed a great many different types of bequests, and you probably feel that you have mentally disposed of about all your estate. However, it is very possible that you have overlooked something. Furthermore, after drawing and executing your will, you may acquire some property in the years to come, and then neglect making provision in your will to cover such acquisition.

Cover property acquired after execution of your will

This contingency may be covered by means of a residual clause. This clause should be placed in your will *even though you do not now feel that it is necessary.*

"All of the rest, residue, and remainder of my estate, of whatsoever nature and wherever situated, I give, devise and bequeath my sister, Mary."

Selecting Your Executor

Considerable care should be given to the selection of an executor. This position is one of great trust, and unless you have complete confidence in the person you select, it might be advisable to have your executor act in conjunction with an attorney, bank or trust company. If so, check with your attorney or bank, to find out if he or it is willing to act either as the only executor, or as a co-executor in conjunction with the executor you intend to name in your will.

Your executor may be either a man or a woman. If a woman, she is referred to as an executrix. It is often a good idea for a husband to name his wife and a banking institution as co-executors. In this way, a wife who possibly lacks business experience will gain by having a bank or trust company to assist her in handling your affairs. This arrangement is often more satisfactory than simply having the bank act alone, since it may lack the familiarity with your business affairs which your wife might have.

Two or more executors

If your estate is of some size or complication, it might be well to name your attorney as a co-executor, instead of a bank. There is no prohibition against having three executors, but this is seldom done unless you are leaving a going business of considerable worth and feel that your wife will need an expert after your death. Also bear in mind that the court will assign executors compensation for their services, payable by your estate. It is more economical to have only one executor.

Executor's bond

Practically all states require the executor to put up a bond to assure the court that he will be responsible to your heirs for any wrongful acts. Of course these bonds cost money and are charged as an expense to your estate. If you are selecting someone with whom you are only moderately well-acquainted (which by the way, is not advisable), you would probably wish him to furnish a bond to the court. However, if you have selected your wife, husband, or close friend, you may want to save the expense of a bond by providing that the executor may serve without putting up a bond.

Your executor should be younger than you

A few considerations about selecting your executor. Of course, if it is to be your wife or husband, that settles any further discussion of the matter for you. However, supposing that you have selected a close personal friend to act as executor, consider his qualifications. A primary consideration is that of age. If your proposed executor is older than you are, he may be expected to die before you do, leaving your estate without an executor. Of course, in that event, the court will place someone in that capacity, but obviously such replacement will not be your choice. Thus, it is wise to select someone younger than yourself.

If you own your own business

Another point to consider in the selection of your executor is business ability, and this is never truer than where you own a business that must be continued or liquidated after your death.

Here are some clauses for your will that may cover your wishes with regard to your executor:

"I hereby nominate, constitute and appoint the Exchange Bank, of New York City, to act as my Executor."

"I hereby nominate, constitute and appoint my wife Ethel as Executrix, of this will, and further direct that she should not be required to post any bond for the faithful performance of her duties."

"I hereby nominate, constitute and appoint my friend, Frank Little, of Sacramento, California, and Frank Callinan, my attorney, of Sacramento, California, to be the co-Executors of this, my last will and testament."

Substitute executor

Now, let us assume that James Smith, the person you have selected, should die before you, or for one reason or another be unwilling to act as your executor when the time comes. A clause may be added to your will providing for a substitute:

"In the event that the said James Smith should predecease me, or should refuse or be unwilling to act as Executor for any reason whatsoever, I hereby nominate, constitute and appoint Ira Franklin as my substitute Executor."

What Do You Want Your Executor to Do?

If you do not give directions to the contrary, most states will require your executor to convert all of the assets of your estate into cash. This may come as a surprise to you, but that is exactly what may happen if you make no provision to the contrary. Of course, you may wish exactly that to be done after your death. If so, it is not necessary to add such instructions or directions to your appointment of an executor.

Continuation of your business by an executor

But it may be that you are the owner of a business you have built up step by step over the years. While it is a going business, it brings in a good income, but if it were to be sold, perhaps it could only be sold for a very poor price, which of course, would mean less money for your family. If you wish your business to continue, you must give directions to this effect. The proper place in your will is immediately following the appointment of your executor.

"I hereby direct that my Executor be, and he hereby is authorized to continue my wholesale grain and produce business, or any part thereof that he should consider advisable, for such length of time as he should deem advisable, bearing in mind the best interests of my estate."

Power to invest and re-invest

It may be that you have unlimited confidence in your executor, and feel that he could do as well as you in handling your business. The following clause may be employed, but ONLY if you have absolute assurance in the complete integrity of your executor:

"I hereby give to my Executor the power to invest and reinvest any funds in my estate; and with full power in such Executor to sell, transfer, exchange, or otherwise dispose of any asset of my estate at public or private sale, in such manner and fashion as he may deem advisable."

Closing Your Will

Lawyers call the end of your will the testimonium clause. Actually, this is very simple, and should read as follows:

"IN WITNESS WHEREOF, I have hereunto set my hand and seal this 21st day of April, 1950."

Draw line for your signature but do not sign at this time

A line should be drawn after this clause for your signature. BUT DO NOT SIGN YOUR WILL NOW. We will take up this matter in the following pages. Do not insert the date in this clause until you are actually ready to execute the will. This is important, since if you do not execute the will on the date that you have filled in you may not correct the date, but will have to recopy the will.

Attestation of Your Will

Attestation actually means the final execution of your will in the presence of witnesses. No will is valid unless properly executed, so be sure to give this matter careful attention both now and at the time of the actual witnessing of your will.

Do not sign your will at this time

Remember, you have not yet signed your will. However, a line has been drawn at the end of your will for your signature. Be sure that the line for your signature is at the physical end of the will.

It is now necessary to add, below the line for your signature, a clause for the witnesses so that a record will exist reciting the circumstances under which the will was witnessed. Requirements vary from state to state, but the following attestation clause is recognized in every state:

"Signed, sealed, published and declared to be the last will and testament of John Parker, the testator above named, in our presence, and at his request, and in his presence, and in the presence of each other, we have hereunto subscribed our names as witnesses this 21st day of April, 1950.

....residing at...
....residing at...
....residing at.."

You have still not signed your will nor had it executed. But be patient, we are only delaying you out of caution, so that you will not commit an error.

Some states require 3 witnesses

Now, as to the number of witnesses, the following states and Puerto Rico require that you have three (3) witnesses to your will:

Connecticut	New Hampshire
Georgia	Philippines
Louisiana	Puerto Rico
Maine	South Carolina
Massachusetts	Vermont

Be safe—have 3 witnesses

All of the remaining states, including the District of Columbia, Alaska and Hawaii, require but two witnesses. However, you may move to a state requiring three witnesses after you execute the will, or you may wish to make provision for the disposition of property located in a state requiring three witnesses. Therefore, three witnesses should be employed.

With regard to the selection of your witnesses, we have now the same general problem that we had with regard to the selection of an executor. The witnesses should be younger than you, if possible, but they should all be over the age of twenty-one. They should also be persons who will not be likely to change their residence with the coming years.

A beneficiary should not be a witness

Please read the following sentence with care: *It is absolutely essential that none of your witnesses be beneficiaries under the terms of your will.* Most courts will void any provision in a will in favor of a person who is also a witness to that will. The rest of the will may be permitted to stand, but the provision in favor of such person will be stricken from the will.

Do not make more than one copy of your will. If you feel that you must have an extra record, copy it into a notebook, with the heading "Unsigned copy of my Will," but do not sign it. Add a statement that it is only for your own convenience and for your own files.

Remember that anyone can be a witness who is over 21 years of age, and who is not a beneficiary under your will. It is all right for a relative or even the executor to be a witness.

The Actual Signing and Execution of Your Will

Assemble your three witnesses in the same room at the same time. Others may be present, but it is advisable to have just your witnesses and yourself present.

You need not reveal the contents of your will

You should now produce your will, and state to the witnesses that you are requesting them to witness your will, and that the document that you are exhibiting is your will. It is not necessary for you to show them the contents of the will, nor to disclose to them any of the terms contained in it.

Sign in ink

If all three agree to act as your witnesses, you are now ready for the actual moment of signing. You will sign your name in the place provided immediately following the testimonium clause and just above the attestation clause. (Don't be worried about these names; they are the clauses we have discussed in the previous pages.) You should sign so that all three witnesses actually see you signing your name. Both you and your witnesses should sign your names with ink.

Your signature and those of your witnesses should be on the same page

It is essential that the attestation clause for the witnesses should be on the same page as your signature, which you have just placed at the end of your will. Therefore, if your will is longer than one page (and it might run on for several pages) you should be careful to see that both your signature and those of the witnesses are on the very same page. If your will is longer than one page, it is well to initial each page by simply writing your initials on the left hand margin of each sheet of your will. Be sure to fill in the date in the attestation clause if you have not already done so.

The witnesses are now ready to sign their names and their addresses in the places provided. There is no particular order in which the witnesses sign. The important thing to remember is that all the witnesses and yourself should stay in the same room until you and your three witnesses have signed. Everyone should watch while everyone else signs. Be sure the witnesses fill in their addresses after the words "residing at."

Place executed will in a safe place

When this little ceremony has been completed, your will has been executed. After thanking your witnesses you should give careful thought as to where to keep your will. A safe deposit box is the best place, but if one is not available, another safe place will do.

After Your Death

Probating your will

Don't be too shocked by the heading of this chapter. First of all, a very long time may elapse before your will is probated. "Probated" means the filing of a will in the court which has charge of the estates of deceased persons. In addition, since we must all die eventually, the wise person recognizes this fact and prepares for it in advance. Your preparation of a will is indicative of your sound judgment in preparing for the inevitable.

Inform your executor of location of will

Now visualize the situation in which your executor is placed after your death. He probably knows that he has been so appointed, as you undoubtedly told him of this fact. But he will have to hunt for your will, unless it is in your safe deposit box, or unless you have told him where to look for it. Therefore, after the execution of your will you should advise him where you plan to keep your will.

After your death, your executor (or executors) will probably call together all the beneficiaries named in your will if they are located within a reasonable distance of each other. If not, he may advise them by letter of their respective shares in your estate. If the beneficiaries live fairly close to one another it is the custom to call them together and read to them the terms of the will. In this way, they become acquainted with the various bequests left them.

Locating estate assets

Your executor is then faced with the problem of assembling your assets. Supposing you own certain stocks or bonds, or have cash in several banks. Will your executor be able to find them? If he is diligent, he will uncover them in time, but certainly the easiest way is to prepare a list of assets and pin it to your will.

Keep important papers near your will

Any other valuable documents that will assist your executor should also be kept with your will. These would include, among others, a birth or baptismal certificate, social security card, marriage or divorce certificate, naturalization and citizenship papers, and discharge papers from the armed forces. This last is particularly important if you wish to be buried in a national cemetery, which is the privilege of every veteran.

It may be that you own a family cemetery plot. By all means keep the deed to such plot with your will, so that your executor will see it. This will prevent his purchasing a cemetery plot, for which funds would have to come out of your estate. Another possibility is that you belong to some lodge or organization which has death and cemetery benefits; your membership certificate should be filed with your will.

Changing Your Will

Wills may be destroyed by tearing or burning

Once a will has been made, it will continue in effect until you change it. Should you destroy your will by burning or tearing it, then you will have no will at all, and you will be in exactly the same position you were in before you made and executed your will.

If you find as the years go by that you wish to change your old will extensively, it is advisable to write a completely new one, and the new will should of course contain the clause canceling all previous wills. This matter was discussed in the section entitled "Canceling a Previous Will." Be very careful to destroy your old will completely.

But suppose you are satisfied with your old will, even though many years have passed. However a person to whom you had intended to leave an oil painting has died and you have now determined to leave it to another friend. You are at liberty to write a completely new will, if you should so wish. If you decide to do so, the new will must be executed with the same formalities and ceremony that governed the execution of your original will.

Making small changes in your will

An easier way to make this or any other small change in your will is by means of a codicil. A codicil is an instrument which changes the terms of a will in one fashion or another.

A sample codicil

The best way to show you what it is like is to give you an example:

"I, Leonard Armin, of the County of Kings, City of New York, State of New York, do hereby make, publish and declare this Codicil to my Last Will and Testament:

I hereby ratify each and every provision of my will executed the 21st day of April, 1950, except insofar as such will is inconsistent with the terms of this instrument.

I hereby cancel my bequest to my good friend, Joseph Malden, now deceased, of the oil painting by the artist, Franz Hals, which is in my library, and give it instead to my friend, Vera Corcoran.

IN WITNESS WHEREOF, I have hereunto set my hand and seal this 17th day of June, 1951.

....

Signed, sealed, published and declared to be a Codicil to the Last Will and Testament of Leonard Armin, the testator above named, in our presence, and at his request, and in the presence of each other, we have hereunto subscribed our names as witnesses this 17th day of June, 1951.

....residing at.....................................

....residing at.....................................

....residing at.............................. "

Sample clauses for a codicil

The above example shows just about how your codicil should read if you wish to change a specific bequest. If you wish to modify a general bequest, you may substitute the following clause in place of the third paragraph above describing the new beneficiary of the oil painting:

"I hereby direct that instead of my good friend, Allen Ormsby, receiving the sum of Seven Hundred and Fifty ($750.) Dollars, he is to receive the sum of One Thousand ($1,000.) Dollars."

This paragraph will change your executor, should you so desire:

"I hereby direct that Murray Parmalge be substituted as my Executor, in place of David P. Vandermeer."

Or to completely eliminate a paragraph of your will:

"I hereby direct that all of clause Five (5) of my will shall be stricken out, and be null and void, which said paragraph refers to a bequest of Five Hundred ($500.) Dollars to John L. Schumacher."

Please bear in mind that the *entire* codicil described above must be employed, except that you may substitute one or more appropriate paragraphs in place of the one with regard to the oil painting used in the sample codicil.

Requisites for executing a codicil

A codicil must be executed and witnessed with the same formality followed in executing and witnessing the will. That means that you must round up three witnesses, either the same ones, or different ones. You must announce to your witnesses that this instrument is a codicil to your will. Be sure to review and follow the procedure outlined previously for the execution of your will. Your witnesses must see you sign, and every one must watch everyone else sign, and no one is to leave the room during this procedure.

The codicil may be written or typewritten on plain paper. However, once executed, it should be treated with the same respect as your will. A good procedure is to fasten the codicil to the will, by paper clips, or other method.

Avoid unnecessary changes in your will

Try to avoid changing or adding codicils to your will if you possibly can. You will help yourself, your heirs, and executor, if you give thought to your bequests *before* you write your will. Don't be the impulsive sort of a person who changes his will every week. Of course, if some person mentioned in your will dies, you have no choice but to add a codicil or to write a new will.

Never correct a will

Wills may not be altered by corrections. It is not possible to change the terms, amounts, or beneficiaries of your will by writing over any part of your will. If you discover an error in your will, or if you wish to change any part of it, write your will over again, being sure to comply with all of the formalities discussed previously.

If Your Estate Does Not Have Enough Assets

An unpleasant thought, but one that cannot be overlooked, is the possibility that your estate may not have assets enough to pay all the bequests you have set forth in your will. It may be that financial reverses have wiped out some of the funds you intended for the purpose of charitable gifts, and so forth. However, your primary obligation is to provide for your wife or husband and your children.

Let us suppose that at the time you execute your will, you are worth $50,000. Your will recites that your various friends and certain charities are to receive a total of $10,000, set forth in various specific and general bequests. You have provided that your wife and children are to receive the remainder of your property by employing a residual clause as discussed in a previous chapter.

But suppose that at the time of your death, your estate is worth only $12,000 instead of the $50,000 it was worth when your will was written. Your friends and charities will receive the $10,000 you provided for them, but your wife and children will get the "residue and remainder" of your estate which in this case comes to only $2,000. Certainly, this is not what you intended when you wrote your will, yet that is exactly what can happen. Of course you can avoid this possibility by changing your will, or by executing codicils as your financial situation changes, but if you fail to do this, your family will suffer.

Provide for this possibility, no matter how remote

You may provide for this contingency by inserting the following clause in your will at any appropriate place. Of course, you should change the percentage to suit your own personal judgment.

"Anything contained in this will and testament to the contrary notwithstanding, should the total of bequests made to my friends and to charities contained in Paragraphs Five, Six and Seven exceed twenty percent (20%) of the gross value of my estate, then and in that event, I hereby direct my Executor that all such bequests to my friends and to charity be abated proportionately, so that they all together shall not exceed twenty percent (20%) of my gross estate."

Property Which Cannot Be
Transferred by a Will

There are several things of value which cannot be transferred to a beneficiary under the terms of a will. Let us consider these items one by one, and consider in each case the reason why such property may not be disposed of under a will.

Pensions

Most pensions are payable directly to a person during the life of that particular person. Any attempt to transfer such pension will be null and void. Some pensions are transferred by law to the widow of the beneficiary of the pension, and some are continued in favor of minor children. The important thing to realize is that you may not give your pension to anyone except the person to whom it will go in any event. The very best procedure is not to mention it in your will at all, but to attach a brief description of the type of pension to your will so that your executor will be able to investigate the matter.

U.S. Government Savings Bonds

Examine carefully your government bonds and find out exactly to whom they are payable. You will find that most of them are payable to the person who originally bought them and then to another person on the death of the original purchaser. These bonds cannot be transferred to anyone else by a will. As the bonds stand, only the parties named may receive the proceeds. In order to have the bonds pass to another person by your will, the bonds must be made out in your name alone, or in the name of your estate. That is, "Payable to the Estate of Ethel O'Donnell," for example.

Dower and curtesy and right of election

These phrases refer to the fact that in many states you may not leave your husband or wife less than a certain specified portion of your estate. They will be discussed in greater detail in a later section.

Community property states

Arizona, California, Hawaii, Idaho, Louisiana, Michigan, Nebraska, Nevada, New Mexico, Oklahoma, Oregon, Pennsylvania, Texas and Washington have so-called "community property" laws. If you reside or own property in those states or in Hawaii, you should read the material covering this subject in a subsequent chapter.

Life insurance policy proceeds

The situation here is quite similar to that involving U. S. Government bonds. When you originally took out your insurance policy, you were required to specify the beneficiary of such policy. If you named your estate as the beneficiary, you may specify in your will the person to whom you wish the proceeds of the policy paid. However, if the policy states that it is payable to a particular person, you may not change the beneficiary by so providing in your will. The proper method of handling this is by changing the beneficiary of your insurance policy. This is usually accomplished by notifying your insurance company and filling in whatever forms it may require.

Property mutually owned

A common example of property owned by two or more people is the private home of a husband and wife. Take out the deed and examine it carefully. If the title is in the name of "Fred and Irma Waters, husband and wife, by the entireties," or ". . . husband and wife, or the survivor thereof," or some similar phrasing, you have a situation involving mutually owned property. If one of these persons named in a deed should die, the survivor becomes the owner of the property which was formerly owned by both. The title is said to pass by law, and you cannot transfer title to this property by anything in your will. But if the deed reads ". . . as joint tenants" after the names, your will can convey title to your undivided half ownership of the property. This may be done by a specific bequest or by a residual clause.

Problems of Disinheritance (Wife or Husband)

If you are legally married, your husband or wife is usually entitled to a share of your estate, regardless of whether you want him or her to have it. There are certain exceptions to be considered, but in general, the surviving husband or wife inherits a part of your estate. Although the amount may vary from state to state, it roughly ranges from about one-third to as much as one-half of the value of the estate in question. Of course, if you live in one of the fourteen states that have community property laws, a different situation is encountered. This will be discussed later.

Since the laws vary between states, you should read the next section with care if it is your intention to disinherit your husband or wife.

Husband's rule regarding real property

Let us take up the problems of husbands first. Bearing in mind the difference between real and personal property, we find that a husband may disinherit his wife from any share in his *real property* in the following states: Alabama, Arizona, District of Columbia, Florida, Georgia, Michigan, North Carolina, North Dakota, South Carolina, South Dakota, Utah and Wisconsin.

Husband's rule regarding personal property

A husband may disinherit his wife from *personal property* in these states: Alaska, Arizona, Delaware, Florida, Georgia, Michigan, New Jersey, North Carolina, North Dakota, Oregon, Rhode Island, South Carolina, South Dakota, Utah and Wisconsin.

Wife's rule regarding real property

The laws are not nearly so liberal to wives who want to disinherit their husbands. For example, a wife may disinherit her husband from her *real property* only in North Dakota and South Dakota.

Wife's rule regarding personal property

A wife may disinherit her husband from *personal* property in these states: Alaska, Delaware, Georgia, New Jersey, North Dakota, Oregon, Rhode Island, South Carolina, South Dakota and Utah.

As a practical matter, however, it is only rarely that a husband or wife wishes to disinherit the other. The problem usually arises when a husband and wife are living separately but are not legally separated or divorced.

Disinheritance presents a difficult problem

The problem of disinheriting a husband or wife is undoubtedly one of the most difficult problems that can face the person drafting a will. Even lawyers feel that a disinheritance is unwise and usually try to persuade their clients against it. For this reason, unless you have a decree of divorce in your hands, do not attempt to disinherit your husband or wife. If you feel that you must do so, it is especially advisable to consult an attorney on this point.

If you have actually received a court decree divorcing you from your husband or wife, it is advisable to state:

"I hereby direct that no part of my estate shall go to my former wife, since I have been awarded a decree of divorce from her in the Supreme Court of the County of Queens, State of New York, on the 19th day of January, 1945."

In this case you should place a certified copy of the court's decree of divorce next to your will. This will be of great assistance to your executor.

Marriage after the execution of your will

But suppose you execute your will while you are unmarried. If you marry *after* the execution of your will, you will undoubtedly be disinheriting your husband or wife, in effect, since it is unlikely that he or she was mentioned in your will. The same logic applies to children born after the execution of the will. Since they have not been mentioned in the will (obviously impossible since they were not born at that time) you have therefore disinherited your child, or children. The correct procedure is to prepare a new will immediately after marriage, or after the birth of a child or children.

Problems of Disinheritance Continued
(Children and Others)

In Louisiana, you may not disinherit your children. In every other state, it is permitted providing certain formalities are carefully complied with. In general, these formalities require you to show in your will and by affidavit, that you knew you were disinheriting your child, or children. This may be accomplished by a simple statement.

In order to disinherit children they should be mentioned in the will

Let us consider disinheritance of children, point by point. Suppose that you have a wife and two small children, and feel that your wife will make ample provision for your children's maintenance and education. You should, therefore, provide in your will that your wife is to receive the proceeds of the estate directly. In the next paragraph, you should add the following:

"As it is my wish that my wife shall have the entire control of my estate, I have deliberately omitted any provision for bequests to my children, Dorothy and Anne, since my wife will make all necessary provision for them."

Whether you realize it or not, you have actually disinherited your children, even though you are doing it for what you conceive to be their best interests. However, regardless of your motive, it constitutes a disinheritance, and as such, you should carefully mention the reason for so doing. It is a good idea to get up an affidavit giving your reasons once again and in detail, for disinheriting your children.

Now, supposing that even after you have executed your will and the affidavit, you and your wife have another child.

Rule regarding children born after execution of will

As explained above, the law lets you disinherit, only if you are aware that you were doing so at the time of the execution of your will. If you expect to have more children, you should add to the above paragraph:

"This discrimination applies to my children now living, hereafter born to me, or adopted by me."

Upon birth of child after execution of will it should be rewritten

You should be reminded of the question presented in the previous section entitled "Problems of Disinheritance" involving marriage and the birth of a child or children, *after* the execution of your will. You have actually disinherited your children, since they are not mentioned in your will, and this is true even though they were not born at the time you wrote your will. Therefore, upon the birth of any child, you must rewrite your will, unless you have included the above paragraph in your will. Thus it is advisable for you to keep this book for future reference.

But, suppose a child of yours has done something to make you feel that such child should not receive any benefit from your estate; or perhaps you have set a son up in business, or given a daughter a wedding present equal to what you feel is her fair share in your estate. In that event, this might be a sample wording:

"I have intentionally made no provision in this, my Last Will and Testament for my son, Howard, since I have purchased for him his farm in Lancaster County, State of Pennsylvania, in accordance with his wish."

Disinheritance of others than wife, husband or child

Now, let us consider the disinheritance of those other than husband, wife or children. If you have no wife or children, your parents, brothers and sisters have an interest in your estate. You do not have to leave them anything; in fact, you may if you wish leave your entire estate to a charity. It is, however, necessary to add the proper clause to your will, and also to prepare a separate affidavit setting forth your reasons in detail for not giving your estate to family members. Here is an example you may follow, modifying it to fit your own situation:

"I hereby make no provision for my parents since they are both persons of considerable wealth and are not in need; and I also make no provision for my sister, since she has not communicated with me since her marriage, and I have therefore decided to make no provision for her whatsoever."

You should bear in mind that these clauses covering your parents and brothers and sisters are required only if you have no wife or children.

Rule regarding relatives, assuming no immediate members of the family

But, let us suppose further that you have neither wife, nor husband, nor any children, that your parents are both dead, and you have no brother or sister living. You should then include a clause covering your cousins, uncles, aunts, and other relatives, being careful to mention them. In these cases, you should take particular trouble in your various affidavits to indicate that you are aware of their existence, and that you nevertheless, do not wish to leave your estate to them.

Problems of Disinheritance Continued
(Community Property States)

The following states and Hawaii have community property laws in one form or other:

Arizona	Nevada
California	New Mexico
Hawaii	Oklahoma
Idaho	Oregon
Louisiana	Pennsylvania
Michigan	Texas
Nebraska	Washington

Community property defined

Community property laws vary from state to state, but in brief, they are the laws by which property acquired by either the husband or the wife during the time they are married, referred to as "community property," belongs in equal shares to both of them. These laws do not apply to the property which either the husband or wife owned at the time of their marriage, nor do they apply to such other exceptions as property inherited by the husband or wife during their marriage. In effect, the husband and wife equally own half of the amount by which they have increased their worth since the time of their marriage. Since each owns half, it is thus clear that neither can disinherit the other of that half which is already his or hers. All residents of the fourteen states listed at the head of this chapter should read this material carefully.

Another point to consider is that you may subsequently live or own property in a community property state. Be sure to revise your will in accordance with the laws of such state, should this occur.

Release of Obligations Owing to You

Executor has duty to collect all sums due to the estate

All of us at one time or another are called upon to
lend money, particularly to members of the immediate
family. We hope to get the money back, but in any
event, we may not wish to pursue the borrower, or to
sue him. An executor, however, is duty bound to collect
all money owing the estate. If the amount is not paid
on the executor's demand, then he will be required to
sue. If it is your wish that the amount owing to your
estate be paid to it on your death, it is not necessary
to mention it in your will. But if you wish the debt to
be forgiven, and the borrower released, so that the
amount actually becomes a bequest from you to the
borrower, you should so provide:

"I hereby release my friend, Benjamin Griffith from the
indebtedness to me in the sum of One Thousand ($1,000.)
Dollars."

The Question of Survivorship
and Lapsed Legacies

Rule regarding prior death of a beneficiary

We have previously considered changing a will by codicil upon the death of a beneficiary before your own death. Let us now consider how to write the will so that such changes will not be necessary.

Let us take a specific situation. Your will provides for a gift of cash in the amount of $5,000 to a favorite friend of yours. However, after your will is executed, but before your death, this friend dies, leaving two children. The bequest is considered to have lapsed; it will not be paid over to his children. The money that you had intended to go to your friend will be turned back into your residual estate. (Note again the need for setting up a residual clause in your will.)

Method to be employed if you wish gift to go to children of a dead beneficiary

But let us suppose that you actually wish the bequest to go to your friend's family if he should die before you. In that event, the bequest should be worded along the following lines:

"I hereby give, devise and bequeath to my friend, William Mander, the sum of Five Thousand ($5,000.) Dollars, and in the event that he predecease me, the said sum is to go to his heirs."

Special rule in some states regarding child, grandchild, brother and sister

In some states, if you leave money to a *child, grandchild, brother,* or *sister,* and make no provision as to where the money is to go in the event that such beneficiary dies before you, the result may be different. These states assume that since the person named is so close to you in relationship, you would want the money to go to that beneficiary's children, even though you have not so provided in your will. It is not necessary to learn the law of your state in this regard. All you have to do is to set forth your wishes clearly; then it will not be possible for the law of your state to change your wishes. If you are making a bequest to your sister, for example, (remember, this rule applies only to bequests to a child, grandchild, brother or sister), and do not want the bequest to go to her children if she should die before you, word it this way:

"I hereby give, devise and bequeath the sum of Twenty Five Hundred ($2500.) Dollars to my beloved sister, Eunice, providing that she shall survive me, and in the event of her prior decease the said sum is to be paid to my friend, Hiram Ortman, of Binghamton, New York."

Sample clauses

However, if you want the bequest to go to your sister's children in the event of her death before you, set forth your wish along these lines:

"I hereby give, devise, and bequeath the sum of Twenty Five Hundred ($2500.) Dollars to my beloved sister, Eunice, and in the event that she predeceases me, the said sum is to go to her heirs."

Preventing Litigation Involving Your Estate

Prepare will and affidavits carefully
in the event of disinheritance

You should bear in mind that the laws of most states assume that your money will go to members of your immediate family, and unless you execute a will providing otherwise, that is just what will happen to your money. This is why we have covered with care the necessity of mentioning the members of your family and preparing affidavits, should you desire to disinherit them. You may review this in the previous chapters covering disinheritance.

Costs involved in defending litigation
involving your estate

Now, let us suppose that you and your wife were deeply hurt by your daughter's marrying without your consent. You are a man of considerable means, your wife has money of her own, and since you both agree that no provision is necessary for her, you execute a will leaving your entire estate to the Parkside Hospital, a charity, being careful to mention in your will the reason for disinheriting your daughter. Upon your death, your daughter might commence a lawsuit to have your will set aside. The expense of defending such a lawsuit, including attorney's fees, court costs, etc., may be quite substantial, and such expenses will be taken out of your estate. That does not necessarily mean that your daughter's suit to set aside your will is going to succeed, but it will have to be defended, and in the meantime, no money may be paid out of your estate, until the claim is concluded. To avoid unnecessary litigation, your executor may pay some money to the person who is suing. This happens quite often.

A simple method of helping to prevent litigation

You cannot stop someone from suing your estate, no matter what precaution you take. However, if you anticipate trouble with some relative, a wise solution is to give that person a small bequest, and then add a clause which will cut him off from this bequest if he should object to the filing of the will or commence litigation.

Provide for alternative disposal in event of lawsuit

It is essential that you specify where the bequest is to go in the event that the beneficiary does object to your will or litigate your estate. The courts have ruled that unless you so specify, all that you are trying to do is to frighten your beneficiaries into accepting the terms of your will. Regardless of the reason, you should always specify where the bequest is to go should there be any lawsuit.

"In the event that any beneficiary to this will (other than my wife) shall object to its probate, or shall directly or indirectly engage in any contest in connection with this will, in such event,

I hereby cancel and nullify any bequest made in this will to such person, and further direct that such person shall be cut off from any share whatsoever in my estate, and I further direct that the bequest to such person shall be considered as part of my residuary estate."

A wife usually may not be disinherited

Possibly you noticed the words "(other than my wife)" in the above paragraph and wondered why they were there. As we discussed the problems of disinheritance, we learned that usually you may not disinherit your wife without cause, and since she is entitled to a certain minimum amount in any event, you may not add any clause which would cut off the right she already had.

Illegal Bequests

Wills against public policy are void

Your will is examined in court after it is probated. At that time, all provisions considered against "public policy," will be declared void. This includes anything contrary to the general good of the public. Of course certain states are more liberal than others, so that if you wish to make a bequest which is out of the ordinary, or wish to put certain clauses in your will which are uncommon for one reason or another, you should check the law of your state carefully by conferring with your attorney.

Avoid unusual or freakish wills

The courts frown on unusual wills and bequests and often declare them void. For this reason it is advisable to avoid freakish provisions in your will. Do not leave bequests on condition that the beneficiary perform specfied weird, distasteful or humiliating acts.

Restrictions regarding usage of a house

For example, a man who had lived in a certain house during all of his adult life provided that his home be boarded up for twenty years after his death, and then given free of charge for two years to any deserving young married couple. The court recognized the sentimental purpose but felt that the closing of a needed house for twenty years was against public policy.

Restrictions regarding marriage in general

A condition in a will to the effect that a person who has never married shall only receive a bequest providing he or she remains unmarried, is usually against public policy, since it is thought that marriage and the founding of families is to the best interest of society.

Restrictions against marrying a particular person

However, it is often possible to put a restrictive clause in a will canceling a bequest to a person if the beneficiary should marry a particular person whom you name:

> "I hereby direct that in the event that my niece, Amy Phelps, shall marry Oren Atwater, then any bequest contained herein shall be null and void, and I further direct that such bequest shall be given instead to my nephew, Philip Coram."

Rule regarding marriage

While you are not allowed to try to prevent a person who has never married from getting married, you are usually permitted to restrict a person from remarrying a second or third time on pain of losing the gift set forth in your will.

Religious marriage restrictions

It is also possible in some states to provide that your beneficiaries may benefit under your will only if they marry persons of a certain religion. Although prohibitions against marrying outside of certain religious faiths may be declared invalid in the future, they are presently considered valid. Such a clause might read:

"I hereby direct that in the event that my son, Roy, shall marry any person who is not a follower of the Roman Catholic faith, then any bequest contained herein shall be null and void, and I further direct that such bequest shall be paid to my residuary estate."

Provision should be made for alternative disposition

Remember if your will provides that a beneficiary is not to receive a gift unless he complies with a requirement stated in your will, it is important to add a statement as to where the gift is to go in the event that the condition is not fulfilled.

Certain political gifts are void

Certain groups of bequests are invalid, for reasons that are political in nature. For example, any gift to an organization dedicated to the overthrow of the United States government is obviously against public policy. Bequests to the Communist Party are void, and even some bequests to people living in foreign countries have been declared invalid. This was particularly true of gifts to German citizens before World War II, since it was found that these persons were not getting the money—their government was taking it. The same general policy is now followed in some states with regard to bequests made to people residing within the Russian-controlled areas.

Encumbered Property

Mortgaged property

Encumbered property is property on which there is money owing. This may be real estate on which there is a mortgage, or it may be personal property on which there is a lien or chattel mortgage.

Provision to pay off real estate mortgage

Possibly you own a home which has a substantial mortgage and on which large payments have to be made. It is your desire to give the home to your son, but he is a young fellow, just married, and not earning enough money to keep up payments on the mortgage. You therefore wish him to have the house free and clear of any encumbrance, and to have such mortgage paid off out of your estate, feeling that he will be able to maintain the house if there is no mortgage on it. This is the way to direct your executor:

"I hereby give, devise and bequeath to my son, Jerome, the farm on which I now live, and known as Silver Top Farm, in North Branch, New Jersey, to be given to him free and clear of any mortgage which may be on record against this property at the time of my death."

In absence of any special direction, executor will turn over property with mortgage in effect

If you do not include the above provision, your executor is not authorized to do anything but turn over the property subject to any mortgage which may be against the property. In many cases, the beneficiary may be unable to maintain the property and will have no choice but to sell the property immediately. This is obviously not your wish, since if you only want the beneficiary to have cash, you would leave him a bequest of cash.

Therefore you must consider whether or not you wish your beneficiaries to receive property free and clear, or subject to the encumbrances which may be charged to that property.

Personal property is often mortgaged

Remember that not only real estate may have mortgages against it. Often personal property is purchased on the installment plan, and money may be owing to the seller secured by chattel mortgages, or conditional bills of sale. This is particularly likely to be true of much farm equipment and automobiles. You should provide for this, if you so wish:

"I hereby give, devise and bequeath to my son, Jerome, the Case Threshing Machine used on my Silver Top Farm, and which is subject to a chattel mortgage, and I hereby direct my Executor to pay off all charges against the said Case Threshing Machine, so that my son shall receive it free and clear of any liens."

Tax Avoidance on Your Estate

Difference between tax evasion and tax avoidance

Tax *evasion* may be described as not paying your state or federal governments what is due them. Tax *avoidance* is taking legal advantage of the provisions of law to reduce the amount of your taxes. This chapter is intended to show you an important method of reducing the tax on your estate, assuming that you are married.

Most people have taken advantage of recent changes in the federal income tax laws which permit a husband and wife to file a joint return. A joint return may result in substantial savings by placing both parties in lower tax brackets. However, this same Revenue Act makes certain provisions with regard to estate taxes which can also result in a considerable saving.

Tax savings available to your estate

If your estate tax amounts to $40,000 and you can legally reduce the tax to $15,000 by means suggested in this chapter, you have increased your worth by $25,000 just as surely as if you had put $25,000 in the bank. Your family may be $25,000 ahead if you heed the following suggestions. First you should know that, for all practical purposes, the federal exemption on estates is now fixed at $60,000. That means that there is no tax on the first $60,000 value left to your heirs. Of course, for tax computations, you must include the value of your insurance policies, your U. S. Government Savings Bonds, and your share of jointly owned property, even though this property may not be transferred by any provision in your will.

Half of estate may be left to husband or wife

For example, suppose your estate amounts to $250,-000. Deducting your exemption of $60,000 leaves a taxable estate of $190,000. The normal federal tax which your estate must pay amounts to about $47,000. But, to take advantage of the provisions of the Revenue Act, you will leave half of your estate to your husband or wife. You are specifically permitted to leave up to half of your estate to your mate tax free, but it is important that your husband or wife receive this property free of all controls. Practically speaking, it should be such an outright gift so that your husband or wife has complete control of the disposition of the property.

Substantial tax savings available

Now let us examine the tax situation described above. You have left half of your estate, or $125,000, to your husband or wife. To compute the tax, subtract the $125,000 left to your wife. This leaves $125,000 from which the normal $60,000 tax exemption will be deducted, leaving a taxable estate of $65,000, on which the taxes will be about $11,000. Your estate saves

$36,000, or stated otherwise, the value of your estate is increased by $36,000.

This is purely a tax saving

The most important thing to remember is that this is a tax benefit, pure and simple. It does not change anything that has been previously discussed, nor are you forced to change your plans in any way. Further, the law does not say you must leave exactly one-half of your estate to your husband or wife. You may leave more or less, as you wish. But your surviving mate is entitled to a tax benefit on as much as one-half of your estate. If you leave less to him or her, there will be a proportionately smaller benefit as to taxes. If you leave more than half to your mate, normal taxes will be due on any amount above one-half the value of the whole estate.

Tax benefits available only for husbands and wives

It is not necessary, however, for you to add any particular wording to your will in order to receive the tax benefits described above. All that you need to remember is that the benefit cannot be taken if the property is left to a child, father, mother, brother or sister. It is available only to husbands and wives.

Some Duties of an Executor (a partial list)

He must:

1. Locate your will.
2. Carry out any specific funeral arrangements which are set forth in the will.
3. Probate the will and be appointed executor by the Surrogate's Court.
4. Prepare books and records to set forth all estate transactions.
5. Open your safe deposit box.
6. Take over control of all personal property.
7. Liquidate or carry on your business affairs.
8. Ascertain all debts due to the estate and arrange for payment of same.
9. Ascertain all other assets of the estate and arrange for collection of same.
10. Arrange for collection of life insurance payable to the estate.
11. Arrange to transfer all stocks, bonds and other securities from your name to the name of the executor.
12. Arrange for payment of all taxes and other expenses.

13. Have real estate and all personal property appraised for tax purposes.

14. Defend the estate in any litigation should anyone sue the estate.

15. Arrange to pay all legacies to beneficiaries set forth in will.

16. Submit final accounting to the court.

Questions and Answers

During the reading of this book, it is likely that certain questions have been forming in your mind. It is the purpose of this section to present some of the most frequently asked questions, together with their answers.

Q. Is there any difference between a will and testament?

A. There was once a difference, but this is no longer the case. For all practical purposes, any will is known as a Last Will and Testament.

Q. Should my will be filed in any state or government office?

A. Not necessary. The proper place for your will is in a safe deposit box, or other safe place.

Q. Can I make my will more legal by having it witnessed by a notary public?

A. This is neither proper nor desirable. The proper procedure to follow is outlined in the section on the actual Signing and Execution of Your Will.

Q. Should I number each page of my will, and in addition, number each paragraph?

A. Your will is valid even if you don't do this, but it is an excellent idea.

Q. What is a holographic will, and is it valid?

A. A holographic will is one that is entirely handwritten and requires no witnesses. It is valid in some states, but you are strongly urged not to attempt such a will.

Q. How does a blind man execute a will?

A. This may be accomplished by adding a statement explaining the situation in the attestation clause described in a previous chapter. The will should, of course, be carefully read to the blind person.

Q. Should I initial each and every page of my will?

A. This is an excellent idea.

Q. What is meant by the wife's dower?

A. Dower is the right of a wife to a portion of her deceased husband's estate. In most states, a wife may not be disinherited. Her minimum share is generally referred to as her "dower" right.

Q. What is curtesy?

A. This is the equivalent right of a husband to a certain minimum share of his wife's estate.

Q. Why is it necessary to say "give, devise and bequeath" before each bequest?

A. There is a historical background for this. The word "give" means just what it says. However, "devise" refers only to real estate; "bequeath" refers only to personal property. To avoid confusion, you are advised to use the full "give, devise and bequeath" regardless of whether you are making a bequest of real or personal property.

Q. If I leave my home to someone, will he also get the furniture which is in the house?

A. No, not unless you add the words ". . . together with all of the furniture, and other personal property located in such house."

Q. If I have any doubts about my will, what should I do?

A. By all means, see your lawyer. He will clear up any doubts you may have.

Q. Does my will have to be drawn on a legal form the same as the one at the end of this book?

A. It is better to use this form, but you can use any paper at all. You are urged, however, to use the form at the end of this book. Legal forms are available at many stationery stores, should you require another.

Additional Clauses Which May Be Suitable for Certain Wills

Giving entire estate to husband: I hereby give, devise and bequeath to my husband, JOHN, providing he survives me, all of my property, both real and personal.

Giving entire estate to wife: I hereby give, devise and bequeath to my wife, MARY, providing she survives me, all of my property, both real and personal.

Giving home to wife for life, with remainder to children: I hereby give, devise and bequeath my home and all of the land and property appertaining thereto and all of the furniture, household goods and effects of all kinds in and about the same, to my wife, MARY, during the term of her life, and after her decease, to my children, ROBERT and EDNA, their heirs and assigns, in equal shares forever, as tenants in common.

Giving personal effects, books and personal property to wife: I hereby give, devise and bequeath to my wife, MARY, all of my household furniture, pictures, books, clothing, jewelry and other personal property of which I may die possessed.

Omitting gift to son, with justification: I have purposely failed to make any provision in this, my Last Will and Testament, for my son, RODERICK, because after careful consideration, I find that I do not wish to make any gift or bequest to him.

Omitting gift to former wife: I have purposely failed to make any provision in this, my Last Will and Testament, for the benefit of my former wife, MARJORIE, as I no longer have any obligation, legally or morally, to provide for her.

Giving children power to divide personal property: I hereby give, devise and bequeath to my sons THOMAS and EUGENE and to my daughters GERTRUDE and EVELYN, in equal shares, all of my collection of antiques, silverware, porcelain and bric-a-brac, except such as herein specifically bequeathed to other persons. I wish that my children will divide this property as equally as possible, amicably, and that each of the four children will cooperate with each other in making a satisfactory division thereof. If, however, they fail to agree upon such equal distribution, then my Executor, hereinafter named, shall make such distribution as he deems advisable in his sole discretion and the determination of my Executor shall be final and binding upon the children.

Canceling and releasing of advances: At various times I have advanced sums of money to my children and to others named in this Will as beneficiaries. None of my children or other beneficiaries shall be charged with or required to pay any money advanced or loaned to them and that all such loans and advances shall be canceled and released.

Devise of office contents to son: I hereby give, devise and bequeath to my son, JOHN, all of the contents in my office, including furniture, rugs, files and all other personal property contained in the said office.

Proportionate reduction of bequests: In the event that my estate shall not be sufficient to pay the foregoing bequests, I direct that they shall be reduced and abated proportionately.

Gifts made free of inheritance taxes: All of the bequests hereinbefore made in this Will shall be paid or delivered to the beneficiaries named free from inheritance taxes or other charges, without diminution for any reason.

Conveyance of real estate, free of mortgage debt: I hereby give, devise and bequeath my farm, together with all of the buildings situate thereon, located in Tarrington, Connecticut, to my son, WILLIAM, his heirs and assigns, free and discharged from any mortgage which may be in existence thereon at the time of my death, and I request my Executors, hereinafter named, to pay out of my estate any sums necessary to discharge any said mortgage upon the said premises.

Gift to become void if Will is contested: In the event that any beneficiary under this Will shall institute or cause to be instituted, directly or indirectly, any action against me or my Executors, or contest this Will, or be a party to any litigation involving the validity of this Will, or involving any of the bequests herein, I direct that the bequest to such beneficiary shall thereupon terminate and become void, and I further direct that the bequest to such beneficiary shall be considered as part of my residuary estate.

Provision for burial: I hereby direct that upon my death, my body shall be interred in a Roman Catholic Cemetery according to the rites of that Church and I direct my Executor to pay out of my estate the necessary expenses for carrying out this direction.

Provision for cremation: I hereby direct that after my death, my body shall be cremated and the ashes shall be placed in an urn and be placed in a suitable place as selected by my Executor, and I direct my Executor to pay out of my estate the necessary expenses for carrying out this direction.

Instruction to destroy papers and letters: I direct my Executor to examine carefully all of my papers, letters and records and to destroy any or all of them as he shall deem advisable in his sole discretion.

Gift of art collection to museum: I hereby give, devise and bequeath to the Metropolitan Museum of Art in the City of New York my entire collection of Siamese Art Objects, South American Artifacts, Etruscan Pottery and 17th and 18th Century French Paintings, all of which are situated on the third floor of my home at 899 Fifth Avenue, New York City.

Right of first choice in connection with art gift: I hereby direct that upon my death, each of my three grandchildren may first select one art object each from my collection which I have donated to the Metropolitan Museum of Art as set forth in the paragraph above.

Gift to orphan asylum: I hereby give, devise and bequeath the sum of $1,000.00 to the Georgetown Orphan Asylum located in Georgetown, Louisiana, in recognition of the kindness shown to me when I was a boy.

Instruction to continue business: I hereby appoint my son, GREGORY, as Executor of this, my Last Will and Testament, and I hereby expressly authorize and empower my said Executor, if he shall so elect, to continue the operation of any business venture, enterprise or operation in which I am interested at the time of my death during the probate of my estate and, further, authorize him to convey, lease, sell or mortgage any portion of my estate or the whole of it, at either public or private sale, and without securing any order of court therefor, nor shall my said Executor be required to post any bond for the faithful performance of his duties.

Bequests to Executors instead of fees: I have made a bequest to each of my three Executors in the sum of $2,500.00 each, which they shall receive in lieu of the fees which they would have received as Executors.

Federal Estate Taxes

Taxable Estate		Maximum Tax		Minimum Tax	
From	To	Amount	Rate on Excess	Amount	Rate on Excess
0	$ 60,000	0	0%	0	0%
$ 60,000	65,000	0	3%	0	3%
65,000	70,000	$ 150	7%	$ 150	7%
70,000	80,000	500	11%	500	11%
80,000	90,000	1,600	14%	1,600	14%
90,000	100,000	3,000	18%	3,000	18%
100,000	110,000	4,800	22%	4,800	21.2%
110,000	120,000	7,000	25%	6,920	24.2%
120,000	150,000	9,500	28%	9,340	27.2%
150,000	160,000	17,900	28%	17,500	26.4%
160,000	200,000	20,700	30%	20,140	28.4%
200,000	300,000	32,700	30%	31,500	27.6%
300,000	310,000	62,700	30%	59,100	26.8%
310,000	500,000	65,700	32%	61,780	28.8%
500,000	560,000	126,500	32%	116,500	28%
560,000	700,000	145,700	35%	133,300	31%
700,000	810,000	194,700	35%	176,700	30.2%
810,000	900,000	233,700	37%	209,920	32.2%
900,000	1,060,000	266,500	37%	238,900	31.4%
1,060,000	1,100,000	325,700	39%	289,140	33.4%
1,100,000	1,310,000	341,300	39%	302,500	32.6%
1,310,000	1,560,000	423,200	42%	370,960	35.6%

1,560,000	1,600,000	528,200	45%	459,960	38.6%
1,600,000	2,060,000	546,200	45%	475,400	37.8%
2,060,000	2,100,000	753,200	49%	649,280	41.8%

Explanation

Assume a person died leaving a total estate worth $600,000. Assume expenses of $20,000 and the authorized exemption of $60,000, a total of $80,000 that can be deducted, leaving a taxable estate of $520,000.

To find the federal estate tax on this property, take the $500,000-$560,000 bracket. The tax on the first $500,000 (low end of the bracket) is $126,500. The remaining $20,000 of the estate is taxed at the rate of 32%:

	Amount of tax
Estate	
1st $500,000	$126,500
Remaining $20,000 @ 32%	6,400
Total Estate—$520,000 Maximum tax—$132,900	

Various credits are allowable before paying the final tax, notably a credit for state taxes. Credits, however, will not be allowed to reduce the total federal tax to below the minimum shown in the last two columns, in this instance:

1st $500,000	$116,500
Remaining $20,000	5,600
	$122,100

The actual amount due will be $132,900 less any allowable credits, but not less than $122,100.

New York State Inheritance Rates

I Net Estate	II Amount of Block	III Rate of Tax on Block	IV Amount of Tax on Block	V (Cumulative) Total Tax
$ 50,000	$ 50,000	2%	$ 1,000	$ 1,000
150,000	100,000	3%	3,000	4,000
300,000	150,000	4%	6,000	10,000
500,000	200,000	5%	10,000	20,000
700,000	200,000	6%	12,200	32,000
900,000	200,000	7%	14,000	46,000
1,100,000	200,000	8%	16,000	62,000
1,600,000	500,000	9%	45,000	107,000
2,100,000	500,000	10%	50,000	157,000
2,600,000	500,000	11%	55,000	212,000
3,100,000	500,000	12%	60,000	272,000
3,600,000	500,000	13%	65,000	337,000
4,100,000	500,000	14%	70,000	407,000
5,100,000	1,000,000	15%	150,000	557,000

6,100,000	1,000,000	16%	160,000	717,000
7,100,000	1,000,000	17%	170,000	887,000
8,100,000	1,000,000	18%	180,000	1,067,000
9,100,000	1,000,000	19%	190,000	1,257,000
10,100,000	1,000,000	20%	200,000	1,457,000
Any amount exceeding	10,100,000	21%		

Explanation

The above table is indicative of inheritance tax rates in some states, although New York is higher than most. As previously mentioned, partial credit is allowed against Federal Estate Taxes for payments made on account of State Inheritance Taxes. (See following table.)

Assume an estate worth $300,000. The first $50,000 will be taxed at the rate of 2%; the next at $100,000 the rate of 3%, and the remaining $150,000 at the rate of 4%.

Estate	Tax Rate	Tax Amount
1st $ 50,000	2%	$ 1,000
Next $100,000	3%	3,000
Next $150,000	4%	6,000
Entire Estate $300,000		Total tax $10,000

State Tax Credit

Taxable estate equal to more than —	Taxable estate less than —	Credit on amount in 1st column	Rates of credit on excess over amount in 1st column Percent
$ 40,000	$ 90,000	—	.8
90,000	140,000	$ 400	1.6
140,000	240,000	1,200	2.4
240,000	440,000	3,600	3.2
440,000	640,000	10,000	4.0
640,000	840,000	18,000	4.8
840,000	1,040,000	27,600	5.6

Explanation

This table shows the credit that will be allowed against Federal Estate Taxes for payments made on account of State Inheritance Taxes. In the example cited under the New York State Inheritance Rate Table, a state tax of $10,000 was paid on an estate of $300,000, but credit for the entire $10,000 that was actually paid will not be allowed. A credit of $3,600 will be allowed for the first $240,000 of the estate, and a credit of 3.2% of the remaining $60,000 of the estate.

	Credit
1st $240,000	$3,600
3.2% of remaining $60,000	1,920
Total allowable credit	$5,520

A Few Sample Wills

In the next few pages, you will find a sample codicil and sample wills suitable for an unmarried man or woman, a married man and a married woman. This does not mean that you must select your will from this group and follow it in detail. They are included, so that you may see several wills in their entirety. The examples are intended to show you what three different wills might look like. Your own will may be much more detailed and contain many more clauses than these samples. At the end a blank form is reproduced which you may use.

In the Name of God, Amen.

I, *Robert Hastings* of the City of *N.Y. Co. & N.Y. State of N.Y.* being of sound and disposing mind and memory, and considering the uncertainty of this life, do make, publish and declare this to be my last **Will** and **Testament:**

I hereby revoke all testamentary instruments heretofore made and executed by me.

1. Insert your full name here. Do not use nicknames.

2. Revoke all previous Wills even though this is your first will.

3. This is required by law.

4. Insert all specific bequests. Use a separate paragraph for each person to whom you leave specific bequests. However, you may give one or more items in each paragraph.
   Several bequests would go here. There are no general bequests in this Will, but if there were, this would be the correct spot.

5. Residual clause.

6. Name your Executor here. If there are 2 or 3, name them all.

I hereby instruct my Executor to pay my just debts and funeral expenses as soon after my death as may be practicable.

I hereby give, devise and bequeath my automobile, or any automobile which I may own at the time of my death, to my nephew, Donald.

All the rest, residue and remainder of my estate, of whatsoever nature and wherever situated, I give devise and bequeath to my sister, Elinor.

I hereby appoint *Rupert Caldwell*

to be Executor of this my last **Will** and **Testament.**

7. Insert the date here. Make sure it is the date that the Will is actually witnessed.

In Witness Whereof, *I have hereunto set my hand and seal, this* ___30th___

day of ___October___ ___ 1950 ___

8. You sign here, but do not do so until your witnesses are present and actually see you sign.

Robert Hastings

9. Fill in your name again.

Signed, sealed, published and declared to be the Last Will and Testament of *Robert Hastings*
___ the testator above named, in our presence, and at his request, and in his presence, and in the presence of each other, have hereunto subscribed our names as witnesses this ___30th___ *day of* ___October___ ___ 1950 ___

10. Witnesses sign here carefully.

Mary Smith Residing at *12569 Broadway, N.Y.C.*
Frank Jones Residing at *839 E. 57 Street, N.Y.C.*
Thomas Edwards Residing at *119 Summit Ave., Newark, N.J.*

Notice:—Do not make any changes and alterations to this will after it has been executed.

NOTE
ONCE THIS WILL HAS BEEN EXECUTED DO NOT CHANGE OR GO OVER ANYTHING IN THE WILL.

Sample Will of an Unmarried Man or Woman

In the name of God, Amen. I, Robert Hastings, of the City of New York, County of New York, State of New York, being of sound mind and memory, but also aware of the uncertainties of this life, do hereby make, publish and declare this instrument as and for my LAST WILL AND TESTAMENT:

I hereby revoke all testamentary instruments heretofore made and executed by me.

I hereby instruct my Executor to pay my just debts and funeral expenses as soon after my death as may be practicable.

I hereby give, devise and bequeath my automobile, or any automobile which I may own at the time of my death, to my nephew, Donald.

All the rest, residue, and remainder of my estate, of whatsoever nature and wherever situated, I give, devise and bequeath to my sister, Elinor.

I hereby nominate, constitute and appoint my friend, Rupert Caldwell to act as my Executor.

IN WITNESS WHEREOF, I have hereunto set my hand and seal this 30th day of October, 1949.

....

Signed, sealed, published and declared to be the Last Will and Testament of Robert Hastings, the testator above named, in our presence, and at his request, and in his presence, and in the presence of each other, we have hereunto subscribed our names as witnesses this 30th day of October, 1949.

....residing at.................

....residing at.................

....residing at.................

Sample Will of a Married Man

In the name of God, Amen. I, Howard Hendrix, of the City of Chicago, County of Cook, State of Illinois, being of sound mind and memory, but also aware of the uncertainties of this life, do hereby make, publish and declare this instrument, as and for my Last Will and Testament:

I hereby revoke all testamentary instruments heretofore made and executed by me.

I hereby instruct my Executor to pay my just debts and funeral expenses as soon after my decease as may be practicable.

I give, devise and bequeath to my son, Irwin, the sum of One Hundred ($100.) Dollars in full satisfaction of every right and interest in and to my estate; my reason for doing so is that he has completely disregarded my wishes for the past seven years, and has gone off to sea against my wishes, and also since I have not heard from him for the past two years.

All the rest, residue and remainder of my estate, of whatsoever nature and wherever situated, I give, devise and bequeath to my dear wife, Ruth.

I hereby nominate, constitute and appoint my wife, Ruth, as my Executrix, and further direct that she shall not be required to post any bond for the faithful performance of her duties.

IN WITNESS WHEREOF, I have hereunto set my hand and seal, this 10th day of August, 1949.

....

Signed, sealed, published and declared to be the Last Will and Testament of Howard Hendrix, the testator above named, in our presence, and at his request, and in his presence, and in the presence of each other, we have hereunto subscribed our names as witnesses this 10th day of August, 1949.

....residing at.............................

....residing at.............................

....residing at.............................

Sample Will of a Married Woman

In the name of God, Amen. I, Harriet Van Blerigan, of the City of Pittsburgh, State of Pennsylvania, being of sound mind and memory, but also aware of the uncertainties of this life, do hereby make, publish and declare this instrument, as and for my LAST WILL AND TESTAMENT:

I hereby revoke all testamentary instruments heretofore made and executed by me.

I hereby instruct my Executor to pay my just debts and funeral expenses as soon after my decease as may be practicable.

I hereby give, devise and bequeath the sum of Three Thousand ($3,000.) Dollars to my mother, Helen Romre.

If my mother shall predecease me, then I direct that my bequest to her shall lapse, and become a part of my residual estate.

All the rest, residue and remainder of my estate, of whatsoever nature and wherever situated, I give, devise and bequeath to my husband, Franklin.

I hereby nominate, constitute and appoint my husband, Franklin, as my Executor, and further direct that he shall not be required to post any bond for the faithful performance of his duties.

IN WITNESS WHEREOF, I have hereunto set my hand and seal this 5th day of October, 1948.

Signed, sealed, published and declared to be the Last Will and Testament of Harriet Van Blerigan, the testatrix above named, in our presence, and at her request, and in her presence, and in the presence of each other, we have hereunto subscribed our names as witnesses this 5th day of October, 1948.

_____ residing at_____

_____ residing at_____

_____ residing at_____

Sample Codicil

In the name of God, Amen. I, Martin Adams of the City of Milwaukee, State of Wisconsin, being of sound mind and memory, do hereby make, publish and declare this instrument, as and for a CODICIL to my Last Will and Testament:

I hereby ratify each and every provision of my Will executed the 11th day of February, 1946, except insofar as such Will is inconsistent with the terms of this instrument.

I hereby direct that instead of my sister, Mary Adams McCann, receiving the sum of One Thousand ($1,000.) Dollars, she is to receive the sum of Two Thousand ($2,000.00) Dollars.

IN WITNESS WHEREOF, I have hereunto set my hand and seal this 7th day of March, 1951.

Signed, sealed, published and declared to be a Codicil to the Last Will and Testament of Martin Adams, the Testator above named, in our presence, and at his request, and in the presence of each other, we have hereunto subscribed our names as witnesses this 7th day of March, 1951.

_____residing at_____
_____residing at_____
_____residing at_____

Last Will
and
Testament

In the Name of God, Amen.

I, ...

being of sound and disposing mind and memory, and considering the uncertainty of this life, do make, publish and declare this to be my last **Will** *and* **Testament:**

    I hereby revoke all testamentary instruments heretofore made and executed by me.

I hereby appoint...
....*to be Execut*..................*of*
this my last Will and Testament.

In Witness Whereof, *I have hereunto set my hand and seal, this*.. *day of* ....196.........

Signed, sealed, published and declared to be the Last Will and Testament of... *the testat*$^{rix}_{or}$ *above named, in our presence, and at* $^{her}_{his}$ *request, and in* $^{her}_{his}$ *presence, and in the presence of each other, we have hereunto subscribed our names as witnesses this*..............*day of*................................., 196.........

.... *Residing at* ....

.... *Residing at* ....

.... *Residing at* ....

Notice:—Do not make any changes and alterations to this will after it has been executed.